S0-BMX-385

WOMEN'S PROFESSIONAL BASKETBALL

Teamwork:

The

SACRAMENTO
MONARCHS

in Action

Thomas S. Owens
Diana Star Helmer

The Rosen Publishing Group's
PowerKids Press™
New York

8508491

To everyone who has waited or worked for a dream. Here's proof that dreams come true.

Published in 1999 by The Rosen Publishing Group, Inc.
29 East 21st Street, New York, NY 10010

Copyright © 1999 by The Rosen Publishing Group, Inc.

All rights reserved. No part of this book may be reproduced in any form without permission in writing from the publisher, except by a reviewer.

First Edition

Book Design: Michael de Guzman

Photo Credits: pp. 4, 5, 12, 20 © Rocky Widner/WNBA Enterprises, LLC; p. 7 © Reuters/Oleg Popov/Archive Photos; pp. 8, 19 © Nathaniel S. Butler/WNBA Enterprises, LLC; p. 11 © Will Hart/WNBA Enterprises, LLC, (inset) © Rocky Widner/WNBA Enterprises, LLC; pp. 15, 16 © Bill Baptist/WNBA Enterprises, LLC.

Owens, Tom, 1960-
    Teamwork, the Sacramento Monarchs in action /by Thomas S. Owens and Diana Star Helmer.
        p.   cm. — (Women's professional basketball)
    Includes index.
    Summary: Profiles some of the key players on the Sacramento Monarchs professional women's basketball team and describes the team's first year in the WNBA.
    ISBN 0-8239-5245-2
    1. Sacramento Monarchs (Basketball team)—Juvenile literature. 2. Basketball for women—United States—Juvenile literature.
[1. Sacramento Monarchs (Basketball team). 2. Women basketball players. 3. Basketball players.] I. Helmer, Diana Star, 1962- .
II. Title. III. Series: Owens, Tom, 1960-   Women's professional basketball.
GV885.52.S25O94 1998
796.323'64'0979454—dc21   98-16488
                                                        CIP
                                                          AC

Manufactured in the United States of America

Contents

Monarchs Crowned

What a week! On Saturday, June 21, 1997, the Sacramento Monarchs played in one of the first WNBA games. They'd beaten the Utah Starzz in Salt Lake City, 70 to 60. Feeling strong, the Monarchs came home Monday to play against the New York Liberty. But the Liberty beat them, 73 to 62.

On Thursday, the Charlotte Sting came to Sacramento. Sportswriters said the Sting could be **champions** (CHAM-pee-unz). Cheering Sacramento fans told the Monarchs that they were the champions. Monarch Pam McGee listened. She sank 11 of 12 free throws. Teammate Ruthie Bolton-Holifield made five three-point shots. Sacramento beat the Sting, 78 to 70!

◀ The Monarchs worked hard as a team to beat the Charlotte Sting.

5

Sisters of the NBA

The idea for the WNBA started in 1996, when the Olympics were held in the United States. After the U.S. Women's Basketball Team won the gold medal, they traveled around America and met their fans. Basketball fans around the country wanted to see these new stars in their own **league** (LEEG) in the United States.

This led the National Basketball Association (NBA) to create the Women's National Basketball Association (WNBA). They decided that the women would play in the same cities as NBA teams, during the NBA's summer vacation. Sacramento fans were excited to learn that one of the first WNBA teams would be in their city.

Many of the players from the 1996 gold-medal-winning Olympic team now play in the WNBA. ▶

6

A Local Hero

Sacramento fans already knew Pam McGee when the WNBA started. Pam had led the nearby University of Southern California Trojans to two **championships** (CHAM-pee-un-ships). She also starred on the 1984 U.S. Olympic team. Before the WNBA, the United States had no **professional** (proh-FEH-shuh-nul) women's teams. So Pam played for money and prizes in Italy and Spain, and learned to speak Italian and Spanish. Her twin sister, Paula, played basketball with her. But family is still most important to Pam. She always finds time for both family and basketball.

◀ During the Monarchs' off-season, Pam McGee wrote a book, called *Sir Jam a Lot*, which is about a basketball player.

Ruthie Rules!

Ruthie Bolton-Holifield grew up being part of a team: She's from a family of twenty children! "We always found games to play," she says. Ruthie became a strong athlete. In the 1996 Olympics, she helped the United States win the gold medal. She also played professional basketball in Italy for four years. In her first season with the WNBA, Ruthie was the league's second-best player in scoring, and fourth-best in steals. She often shows she's happy by singing for fans—both in English and in Italian!

10

Before joining the Monarchs, Ruthie played professional ▶ basketball in Sweden, Hungary, and Italy.

Time to Help

Chantel Tremitiere has fourteen brothers and sisters in her family. She started playing basketball because her family needed another player to make two even teams. Like her, eleven of her brothers and sisters are **adopted** (uh-DOP-ted). That's why Chantel formed Assist One, a group that helps kids who need families. Just like her group, Chantel's job for the Monarchs was to provide **assists** (uh-SISTS). As a point guard, she helps her teammates score. For the first season she played an **average** (AV-rij) of 37.8 minutes for every 40-minute game! Chantel spent more time on the court than any other WNBA player.

◄ No matter where the Monarchs play, at least one of Chantel's family members can come to see her play. Chantel's grown-up brothers and sisters live all around the United States.

13

Gordon Is Golden

Growing up, Bridgette Gordon was taller than most boys. So her brother took her to the playground to be on his basketball team. Bridgette loved playing. With the University of Tennessee, she played in four straight Final Four **tournaments** (TOOR-na-ments). The Final Four tournament is one of the most important college basketball tournaments played each year. Her team won two championships. In 1988, she helped Team USA win an Olympic gold medal. In 1989, she started playing professionally overseas. She has her own fan club in Italy. It's called Boys of Bridgette!

Bridgette Gordon played so well in college that her team, the Lady Vols, retired Bridgette's jersey number. That means that no one on the college team will ever wear Bridgette's number again. ▶

A New Leader

The Monarchs' first WNBA season was halfway finished. They'd won five games, but they'd lost ten. Ruthie Bolton-Holifield was injured and couldn't play. And Pam McGee was so unhappy with the coach, she wasn't playing either.

The Monarchs' president, Rick Benner, didn't have much time. So on July 28 he asked **assistant** (uh-SIS-tant) coach Heidi VanDerveer to take over as head coach. Heidi had coached Bridgette Gordon at the University of Tennessee in 1987 and 1988. Heidi was excited to take over as head coach. Her three rules were play hard, play smart, and have fun.

◀ Coaching runs in Heidi's family. Her big sister, Tara, coached the 1996 gold-medal-winning Olympic team.

Stop the Streak

The Monarchs had a new coach. Ruthie Bolton-Holifield and Pam McGee came back to play. But the team's losing streak continued. Seven games were lost—then eight—then nine. No WNBA team had ever lost so many games in a row.

The Monarchs met the Sting again. Charlotte was close to earning a spot in the **play-offs** (PLAY-offs). But "We just kept playing," Ruthie says. "We didn't give up." Ruthie hit four 3-point baskets, and scored 24 points. The Monarchs' bad luck ended with a 77 to 64 win over the Sting!

It took a little time to get organized, but with Heidi in charge the Monarchs finally ended their losing streak. ▷

Real Winners

After the losing streak, the Monarchs won four in a row. Then they lost four more, including their last home game. More than 10,000 Sacramento fans were there. But when that game was over, fans cheered for 30 minutes. The arena seemed like a party. Players sang with the fans. They threw **autographed** (AW-tuh-graft) jerseys and shoes to the crowd. Later, the Monarchs and some of the fans went to a restaurant. Some fans gave gifts to their favorite players. The game was a loss, but the season was a win!

◄ After Sacramento fans cheered their Monarchs, Coach VanDerveer said, "You couldn't help but be excited for the future of this team and the city."

Monarchs Keep Flying

During the first WNBA off-season, Ruthie Bolton-Holifield joined NBA Sacramento King player Mitch Richmond to play 2Ball, a basketball skills contest held before the NBA All-Star game. Ruthie helped prove that men and women can play well together. The fans keep helping too. "It's good to know the fans are there," Ruthie said. "They cheered us at the end, and that will motivate us to come back and have a better season next year." It's almost as if the players and fans are teammates. When the players have fun, the fans do too.

Web Sites:

You can learn more about women's professional basketball at these Web sites:

http://www.wnba.com
http://www.fullcourt.com

Glossary

adopt (uh-DOPT) To take a child with other parents and bring him or her up as part of your family.

assist (uh-SIST) Passing to a teammate so that she can score.

assistant (uh-SIS-tant) A person who helps.

autograph (AW-tuh-graf) The signature of a famous person.

average (AV-rij) The usual amount of something, such as the usual amount of points one player scores in a basketball game.

champion (CHAM-pee-un) The winner.

championship (CHAM-pee-un-ship) The last game of a season that determines which team is the best.

league (LEEG) A group of teams that play against one another in the same sport.

play-offs (PLAY-offs) Games played by the best teams at the end of the regular season to see who will play in the championship game.

professional (proh-FEH-shuh-nul) An athlete who earns money for playing a sport.

tournament (TOOR-na-ment) When a large number of teams play against one another in a short amount of time.

Index

A
adopt, 13
assist, 13
assistant, 17
Assist One, 13
autograph, 21
average, 13

B
Benner, Rick, 17
Bolton-Holifield, Ruthie, 5, 10, 17, 18, 22

C
champion, 5
championship, 9, 14
Charlotte Sting, 5, 18

F
Final Four tournament, 14

G
Gordon, Bridgette, 14, 17

L
league, 6, 10

M
McGee, Pam, 5, 9, 17, 18
McGee, Paula, 9

N
National Basketball Association (NBA) 6, 22
New York Liberty, 5

O
Olympics, 6, 9, 10, 14

P
play-offs, 18
point guard, 13
professional, 9, 10, 22

R
Richmond, Mitch, 22

T
Tremitiere, Chantel, 13

U
Utah Starzz, 5

V
VanDerveer, Heidi, 17

24